TENNESSEE TITANS

BY TODD KORTEMEIER

abdopublishing.com

Published by Abdo Publishing, a division of ABDO, PO Box 398166, Minneapolis, Minnesota 55439. Copyright © 2017 by Abdo Consulting Group, Inc. International copyrights reserved in all countries. No part of this book may be reproduced in any form without written permission from the publisher. SportsZone™ is a trademark and logo of Abdo Publishing.

Printed in the United States of America, North Mankato, Minnesota
042016
092016

THIS BOOK CONTAINS RECYCLED MATERIALS

Cover Photo: Jeff Haynes/AP Images
Interior Photos: Jeff Haynes/AP Images, 1; Al Messerschmidt/AP Images, 4-5; Wade Payne/AP Images, 6-7; David F. Smith/AP Images, 8-9; AP Images, 10-11, 12-13, 18; NFL Photos/AP Images, 15; Ed Kolenovsky/AP Images, 14; Tom DiPace/AP Images, 16-17; David Durochik/AP Images, 19; Jake Herrle/AP Images, 20-21; Mark Humphrey/AP Images, 22-23; Paul Spinelli/AP Images, 25; Mark Cowan/Icon Sportswire, 24; John Russell/AP Images, 26-27; James Kenney/AP Images, 28-29

Editor: Patrick Donnelly
Series Designer: Nikki Farinella

Cataloging-in-Publication Data

Names: Kortemeier, Todd, author.
Title: Tennessee Titans / by Todd Kortemeier.
Description: Minneapolis, MN : Abdo Publishing, [2017] | Series: NFL up close | Includes index.
Identifiers: LCCN 2015960448 | ISBN 9781680782363 (lib. bdg.) | ISBN 9781680776478 (ebook)
Subjects: LCSH: Tennessee Titans (Football team)--History--Juvenile literature. | National Football League--Juvenile literature. | Football--Juvenile literature. | Professional sports--Juvenile literature. | Football teams--Tennessee--Juvenile literature.
Classification: DDC 796.332--dc23
LC record available at http://lccn.loc.gov/2015960448

TABLE OF CONTENTS

MUSIC CITY MIRACLE 4

HOUSTON YEARS 8

EARL AND BUM 12

WARREN MOON ERA 16

BECOMING TITANS 20

DECLINE AND FUTURE 26

Timeline 30
Glossary 31
Index / About the Author 32

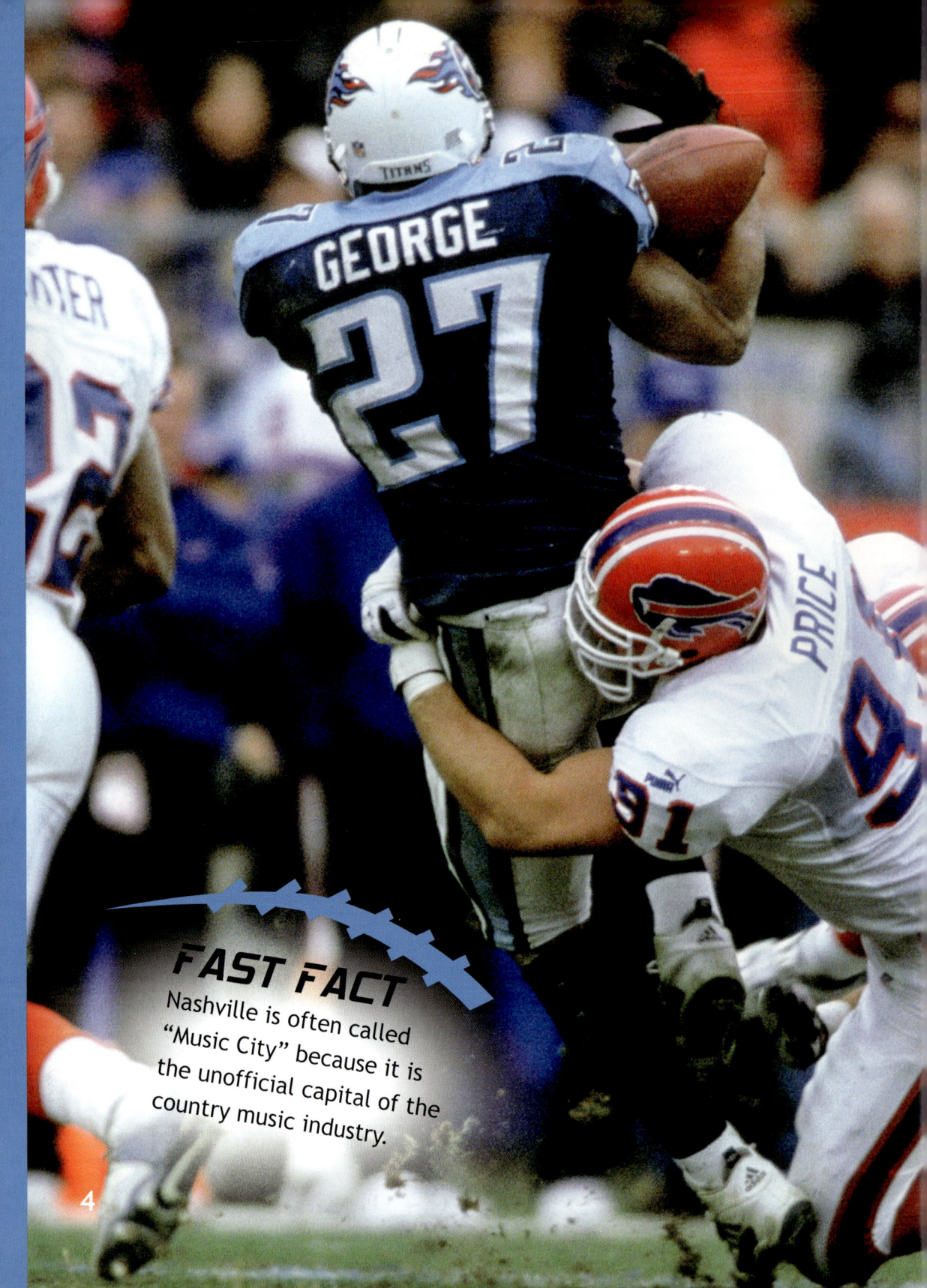

FAST FACT
Nashville is often called "Music City" because it is the unofficial capital of the country music industry.

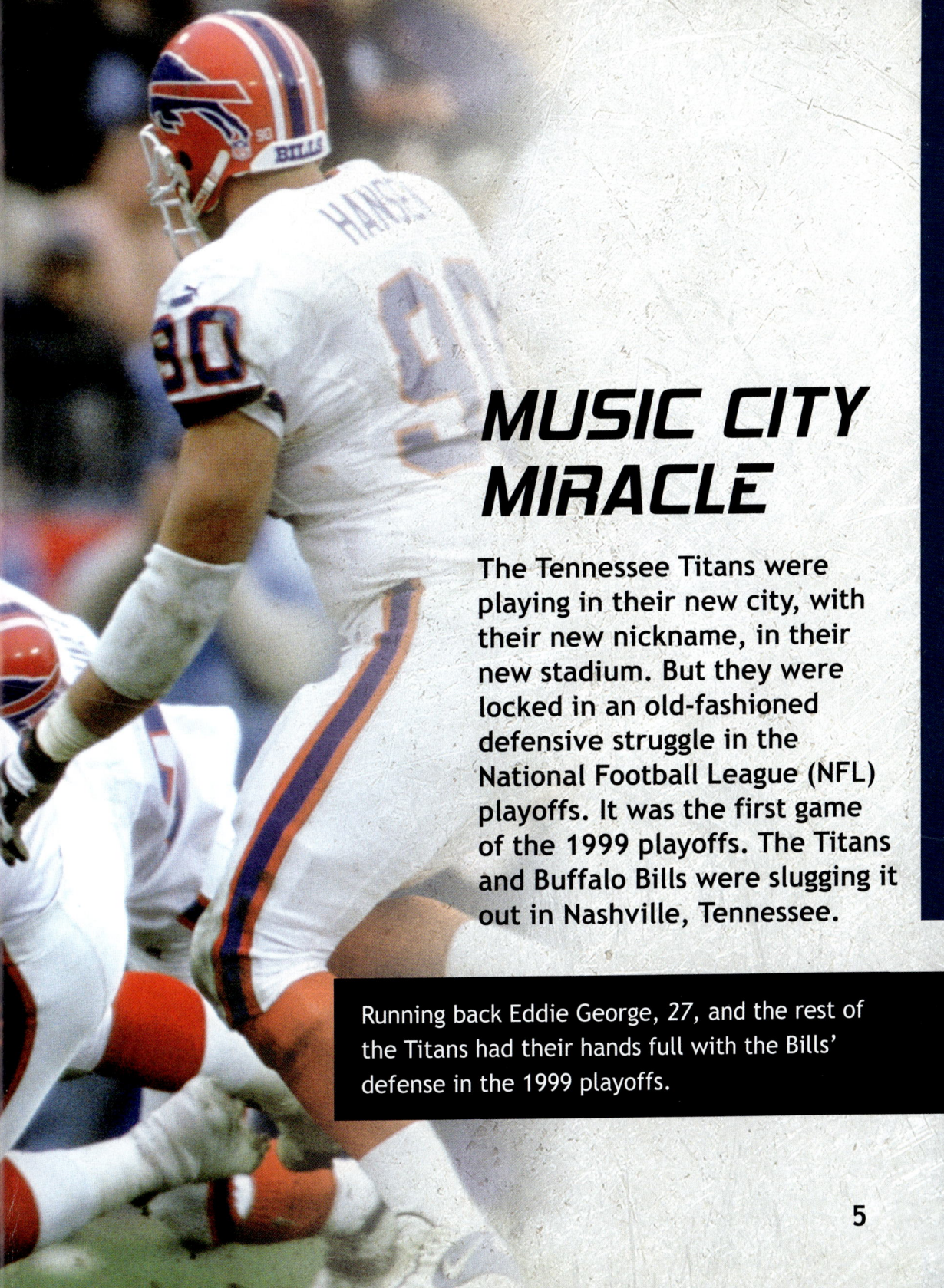

MUSIC CITY MIRACLE

The Tennessee Titans were playing in their new city, with their new nickname, in their new stadium. But they were locked in an old-fashioned defensive struggle in the National Football League (NFL) playoffs. It was the first game of the 1999 playoffs. The Titans and Buffalo Bills were slugging it out in Nashville, Tennessee.

Running back Eddie George, 27, and the rest of the Titans had their hands full with the Bills' defense in the 1999 playoffs.

The teams traded field goals late in the fourth quarter. The second one gave the Bills a 16-15 lead with only 16 seconds left. The Titans' last hope was to make something happen on the kickoff return. Fullback Lorenzo Neal caught the ball. He handed it off to tight end Frank Wycheck. Then, Wycheck turned and threw a lateral across the field to wide receiver Kevin Dyson. Dyson took off down the sideline 75 yards for the game-winning touchdown.

Titans 22, Bills 16. The play became known as the "Music City Miracle." It was the first playoff win for the Titans in their new home. Their last playoff victory had come in 1991, when they were the Houston Oilers. But there were even bigger wins to come.

FAST FACT

Officials reviewed the play and determined it was legal. But many Bills players still believe Wycheck's throw was a forward pass, which would have been illegal.

Kevin Dyson, *87*, gets an escort from his teammates as he races to the end zone to beat the Buffalo Bills.

HOUSTON YEARS

The Tennessee Titans began life in Houston as the Oilers. They were original members of the American Football League (AFL), which began play in 1960. The Oilers were one of the AFL's best teams. They won the league's first two championships. They narrowly missed a third in 1962, losing to the Dallas Texans in double overtime in the title game.

Oilers running back Billy Cannon catches a pass against the San Diego Chargers in the 1961 AFL Championship Game.

FAST FACT
The 1962 AFL Championship Game was, to that point, the longest game in pro football history. It lasted 77 minutes, 54 seconds.

Oilers quarterback George Blanda drops back to pass against the New York Jets in 1965.

Hall of Famer George Blanda was the Oilers' quarterback from 1960 through 1966. He and wide receiver Charlie Hennigan were responsible for a lot of Oilers yards during that time. Hennigan caught 101 passes in 1964. It was a professional football record that stood for 20 years.

FAST FACT

The Oilers played their first five years at Jeppessen Stadium and the next three years at Rice Stadium. In 1968, they moved indoors to the Houston Astrodome.

EARL AND BUM

The AFL merged with the NFL at the start of the 1970 season. But the Oilers' AFL success did not immediately carry over to their new league. Despite the efforts of quarterback Dan Pastorini, the Oilers did not post a winning record until 1975. Included in that stretch were back-to-back 1-13 seasons. The 1973 team was outscored 447-199.

Fortune changed for the Oilers in 1978 when they drafted running back Earl Campbell.

FAST FACT

O. A. "Bum" Phillips was the coach behind the Oilers' resurgence. His son, Wade Phillips, later became an NFL head coach.

Bum Phillips, *right*, coached the Oilers to a winning record five times in his six seasons in Houston.

Campbell had won the Heisman Trophy while playing for the Texas Longhorns just up the road in Austin. He became one of the best running backs in the NFL right away. He won the NFL Most Valuable Player (MVP) Award in each of his first two seasons. He led the league in rushing in each of his first three seasons.

The Oilers made the playoffs three straight years after Campbell's arrival. They reached the conference championship game twice. But they could not break through to their first Super Bowl.

Earl Campbell ran with a unique combination of speed and power.

Dan Pastorini was the Oilers' starting quarterback throughout the 1970s.

FAST FACT

Four players from the 1970s Oilers made the Pro Football Hall of Fame: Earl Campbell, safety Ken Houston, and defensive linemen Elvin Bethea and Curley Culp.

WARREN MOON ERA

While the Oilers remained a strong rushing team with Earl Campbell, their passing game was inconsistent. In 1984, a quarterback named Warren Moon joined the Oilers from the Canadian Football League. In his first season, Moon threw for 3,338 yards. That set a new team record. Moon went on to break that record four times.

After winning five league titles in Canada, Warren Moon returned to the United States and led the Oilers to more playoff success.

Campbell was traded for a draft pick during the 1984 season. Moon became the leader on offense, along with great receivers such as Drew Hill and Haywood Jeffires. In 1986, new Oilers coach Jerry Glanville changed the team's offense to take advantage of Moon's abilities. The result was seven straight playoff appearances from 1987 through 1993.

Moon set several passing records in his Hall of Fame career, but he did not lead the Oilers to the Super Bowl or even a conference championship appearance.

Jerry Glanville, *left*, was the Oilers' feisty head coach from 1985 through 1989.

Haywood Jeffires led the NFL with 100 receptions in 1991.

FAST FACT
Oilers offensive linemen Mike Munchak and Bruce Matthews went on to the Hall of Fame. These teammates were key pieces of the 1980s and 1990s Oilers teams.

BECOMING TITANS

Disgruntled with the aging Astrodome, Oilers owner Bud Adams started looking for a new home for the team in the mid-1990s. That home turned out to be Tennessee, where the Oilers moved in time for the 1997 season. They played as the Oilers for two seasons before changing their name to the Titans before the 1999 season.

FAST FACT

The Oilers played the 1997 season at the Liberty Bowl in Memphis. In 1998, they played at Vanderbilt University's stadium in Nashville.

The Oilers had a hard time drawing fans to games at the Liberty Bowl in 1997, but that changed when they moved into their new stadium in Nashville.

FAST FACT

The team dropped the Oilers name because it had no connection to Tennessee. In the early days of the AFL, the New York Jets were named the Titans.

The Titans still had a core group of talent from their Houston days. Coach Jeff Fisher, quarterback Steve McNair, and running back Eddie George all began their careers in Houston. But they really took off in Nashville.

Eddie George, *right*, was a bruising running back for the Oilers and Titans for eight seasons.

The 1999 Titans went 13-3 and made it to the Super Bowl for the first time. Facing the St. Louis Rams, they made a fourth-quarter comeback to tie the game at 16-16. But then the Rams scored another touchdown. Tennessee had to match it. The Titans drove down to the 10-yard line with five seconds left in the game.

McNair hit wide receiver Kevin Dyson with a short pass. Dyson reached the ball toward the goal line, but he was stopped short. The Titans lost the Super Bowl by just one yard.

Kevin Dyson kneels dejectedly after the Titans lost to the Rams in the Super Bowl.

Titans wide receiver Kevin Dyson comes up just short of the goal line on the last play of the Super Bowl.

DECLINE AND FUTURE

The Titans made five more playoff appearances under Jeff Fisher. He left after the 2010 season as the winningest coach in team history. Steve McNair and Eddie George continued to be great players for many of those years. George had more than 10,000 career rushing yards, the most in team history.

Tennessee had some strong teams but could not match its success of 1999. Chris Johnson became the starting running back in 2008. He rushed for 2,006 yards in 2009. Hall of Famer Mike Munchak returned to the team as coach in 2011, but they did not get back to the playoffs in three seasons.

Chris Johnson, *28*, used his breakaway speed to lead the NFL in rushing in 2009.

Marcus Mariota throws a pass against the Oakland Raiders during his rookie season in 2015.

In 2014, the Titans had their worst season in Tennessee, going 2-14. But that got them a high 2015 draft pick, which they used on quarterback Marcus Mariota. With Mariota and star receiver Delanie Walker, the Titans hope to make a quick return to the playoffs.

FAST FACT

The Titans have drafted four other quarterbacks in the first round. Dan Pastorini and Steve McNair led them to the playoffs. Vince Young and Jake Locker did not.

TIMELINE

1960
The Houston Oilers begin play in the AFL.

1961
The Oilers win their first championship, defeating the Los Angeles Chargers 24-16 on January 1. They follow that with another title by beating the Chargers 10-3 on December 24.

1978
The Oilers draft Earl Campbell, who is named the league MVP in his rookie season.

1980
For the second straight year, the Oilers fall one game short of the Super Bowl, losing to the Pittsburgh Steelers 27-13 on January 6.

1991
Warren Moon becomes the third quarterback in NFL history to pass for 4,000 yards in back-to-back seasons.

1997
Owner Bud Adams moves his Oilers to Tennessee. They play their first season at the Liberty Bowl in Memphis.

1999
The Oilers change their name to the Titans and open Adelphia Coliseum. They go 13-3 and qualify for the playoffs as a wild card.

2000
The Titans win two road playoff games to reach their first Super Bowl, which they lose to the St. Louis Rams 23-16.

2015
The Titans select quarterback Marcus Mariota with the second pick in the NFL Draft.

GLOSSARY

DISGRUNTLED
Unhappy or dissatisfied.

DIVISION
A group of teams that help form a league.

HEISMAN TROPHY
The award given yearly to the best player in college football.

INCONSISTENT
Up and down; sometimes good, sometimes bad.

LATERAL
A pass that goes sideways or backward.

MERGE
Join with another to create something new, such as a company, a team, or a league.

OVERTIME
An extra period or periods played in the event of a tie.

PLAYOFFS
A set of games after the regular season that decides which team will be the champion.

WILD CARD
A team that makes the playoffs even though it did not win its division.

INDEX

Adams, Bud, 20

Bethea, Elvin, 15
Blanda, George, 10, 11

Campbell, Earl, 12, 14, 15, 16, 18
Cannon, Billy, 8
Culp, Curley, 15

Dyson, Kevin, 6, 7, 24, 25

Fisher, Jeff, 22, 26

George, Eddie, 5, 22, 23, 26
Glanville, Jerry, 18

Hennigan, Charlie, 11
Hill, Drew, 18
Houston, Ken, 15

Jeffires, Haywood, 18, 19
Johnson, Chris, 26, 27

Locker, Jake, 29

Mariota, Marcus, 28, 29
Matthews, Bruce, 19
McNair, Steve, 22, 24, 26, 29
Moon, Warren, 16, 18, 19

Munchak, Mike, 19, 26

Neal, Lorenzo, 6

Pastorini, Dan, 12, 15, 29
Phillips, Bum, 12, 13
Phillips, Wade, 12

Texas Longhorns, 14

Vanderbilt University, 20

Walker, Delanie, 29
Wycheck, Frank, 6

Young, Vince, 29

ABOUT THE AUTHOR

Todd Kortemeier has authored dozens of books for young people, primarily on sports topics. He is a graduate of the University of Minnesota's School of Journalism & Mass Communication. He lives near Minneapolis, Minnesota, with his wife.